Delphi

The Oracle and Sacred Site of Ancient Greece

Table of Contents

Introduction 1

Chapter 1: Delphi, the Navel of the World 3

The Timeline of Delphi 3

Chapter 2: Apollo and His Connection
to Delphi 15

Dionysus 18

Apollo and His Complicated Love Life 19

Male Lovers 22

Branchus 22

Apollo and His Attributes and Symbols 24

Chapter 3: The Oracle of Delphi 27

The Oracle 28

Interpreting the Words of the Oracle 32

Who Could Become a Pythia? 34

Some of the More Momentous Consultations
with the Pythia....................................... 35

Chapter 4: The Great Excavation **40**

    Greek Excavations 42

    The Great Excavation 43

    The Sanctuary of Apollo 46

    The Galaxidi Museum 49

    Chrisso Folk Museum 50

    The British Military Cemetery 50

Chapter 5: The Archaeological Museum
           of Delphi **52**

    The Fourteen Rooms and What
    They Contain 58

Chapter 6: The Delphic Maxims..............................**66**

    Some of the More Recognizable Maxims 69

Conclusion **71**

References..**73**

Introduction

Ancient Greece, the land of the gods and goddesses, was filled with beautiful people and heavenly-looking youths. Greece was the cultural center of Europe and one of the most forward-thinking societies on Earth. Delphi was the place to be when it came to the mysteries of the ancient world. It underwent several stages of development and was the object of interest for many conquering armies. They wanted to be the leaders of such a sacred space where the great oracle known as the Pythia resided and spread the wisdom of the gods. Over several thousand years, the area was subject to attacks, to natural phenomena like earthquakes or fires, and was the site of three Sacred Wars.

In the end, Delphi ceased to exist because of the dawn of Christianity. Its pagan ways were considered archaic until the late nineteenth century, when a resurgence in interest meant that archaeologists across the globe began to recognize the importance of ancient sites.

This is the story of Delphi and her past. Take a deep breath and close your eyes. Imagine the cool Mediterranean breeze on your face and the smell of the arid earth and lush springs that tell your senses you are in Greece. Take a step forward and join the millions of people who have trodden the ancient path to the Temple of Apollo to hear their fates. Imagine what it felt like to wait in line to hear what she had to say about your future, her words coming directly from the god Apollo.

Now you are ready to enter Delphi and drink in the atmosphere, so Kalos irthes sten ellada, or Welcome to Greece.

Chapter 1:

Delphi, the Navel of the World

I n Greek culture, Delphi is the center of the universe and is the meeting point of the eagles set free by Zeus, the god of sky and thunder. Eagles were the prominent bird featured in Greek mythology. They represented the original deity Gaia, the personification of the Earth and the primordial mother of all life. She was worshipped in conjunction with Demeter, with whom she produced her children, including Uranus, the sky god. She then entered into a sexual union with Uranus to produce the Titans, a race of people who then produced the Olympian gods and the Giants. She also bore the god Pontus, god of the sea, and then entered a sexual union with him to bear the primordial sea gods of early Greek mythology.

The Timeline of Delphi

Despite her elevated status, Gaia was traditionally regarded as a chthonic deity who was an underworld figure. In art, she is often portrayed as a matronly woman who is suspended between the Earth and the underworld, often holding an infant. She is the mother of all things in Greek culture and was worshipped as the main deity from 1700BC to 1400Bc at the site of Delphi.

In 1500BC, the site was first settled, and Apollo was believed to have arrived at the site in the following century. Apollo was one of the primary gods in Greek mythology, and one of his primary places of worship was Delphi. Apollo plays a significant part in the chronology of Delphi, and you will read more details about him later.

In 800BC, the site of Delphi is first mentioned in texts referring to it as a religious center and of interest to worshippers. In the following fifty years, the word was spread about its significance beyond the Greek borders and throughout the world.

In 650BC, the first temple of Apollo was constructed from branches of a bay tree. The famous traveler Pausanias wrote in his observations from the second century BC that the temple resembled a hut and was decorated with elaborate laurels from the bay tree. It was built on the site where

Apollo slayed the dragon-style creature known as the Python that resided in the center of the Earth, which was Delphi, according to Greek lore.

Between 595BC and 585BC, the site of Delphi was marred by the first Sacred War when the city of Kirrha formed an army to invade and take over the sacred site. There had already been some conflict between the dwellers of Delphi, who accused the Kirrha people of mistreating the pilgrims en route to Delphi and robbing them as they made their sacred journey. The war ended when the Delphi forces used poison to infect the city's drinking water. The poison was hellebore, and it rendered the population so weak with diarrhea that they couldn't fight anymore. Delphi forces took the city and slaughtered the entire population. There are varying versions of the story of the Sacred War, but the outcome is always the same, Kirrha was defeated.

In 586BC, the first Pythian Games marked the end of the war. The games were named after the slaying of the Python by Apollo, and they became part of the Panhellenic games, which would take place every four years at Delphi. They would be ranked after the Olympic Games in importance, but they were more inclusive and included several events for female athletes. Preparations for the games began six months earlier, and a committee from Delphi was sent to Greek cities to announce the games and attract athletes. They also informed the inhabitants of the cities that the Sacred War was over, and they no longer risked being assaulted or robbed when they visited the site. The declaration was called the Sacred Truce and ensured that the games went well and brought much-needed revenue to Delphi following the war.

580BC saw the sculpting of the Koori Twins of Argos Clovis and Bilton. The figures are oversized naked identical figures with their names inscribed on the base of each statue. They were the oldest archaic forms of funerary statues ever found, and they are still on display today at the museum of Delphi.

560BC, the oracle at Delphi is consulted by King Croesus, the King of Lydia, who was renowned for his wealth. His gifts and offerings can still be found at the site of Delphi, and his story remains one of the most recognized in contemporary literature.

In return for his lavish gifts and patronage of the temple of Apollo, he was granted the sanctuary of Apollo and would have been allowed to consult the oracle in the same way as a Delphian priest. He consulted the oracle in 560BC and was told that if he attacked the Medes, an Iranian race of people who inhabited the area known as Media, he would be destroying an empire.

Despite his former friendly relations with the Medes, he saw this prophecy as a positive sign that he should go ahead with the attack. Croesus had already been successful in campaigns to rule over different peoples, including the Ionians, Cilicians, and the Mysians. His empire was vast, and the kingdom of Croesus gave him immense self-confidence. He was convinced the attack on the Medes would be successful. He was wrong, and the Lydian Empire was no more.

In the same year, the column of the Naxians was constructed on Delphi at the temple of Apollo. The islanders of Naxos dedicated the sphynx to cement their relations in Delphi and to honor their importance in Greek mythology. The island is the largest of the Cyclades Islands and reputedly the home of the teenage Zeus and the place where the sea god Poseidon first spotted his future wife, Amphitrite, as he drove his chariot along the seashore.

525BC saw the construction of the Treasure of the Siphnians, which was built to host the offerings and gifts of the city of Siphnos. It is a small building made from expensive and rare Parian marble and was the first of a trio of treasuries that marked the beginning of the Sacred Way. At the time, Siphnios was one of the most prosperous Greek islands, gaining its wealth from gold and silver mines. The treasury intended to host the opulent votive offerings given by the city's inhabitants.

It is a magnificent representation of Ionic art. It is decorated with friezes on all four sides, which depict the assembly of gods watching the Trojan Wars, the labors of Hercules and Apollo, the rape of the Leukippidai, and the judgment of Paris. The decorations are incredibly detailed and include clarity of form and explosive arrangements that had been lacking before this era.

510BCthe second temple of Apollo was built following a fire that destroyed the first temple.

490BC saw the construction of the treasury of the Athenians, which was commissioned after their victories at Marathon and Persia. The significance of the victories meant that the building symbolized their newly acquired democracy and impressive skills on the battlefield. It housed some of the most important trophies from their military past, alongside loot and offerings they dedicated to Apollo. The building contained magnificent friezes and was decorated with reliefs depicting Hercules's labors and Theseus's adventures. Within the walls, there were hymns dedicated to Apollo and complicated political resolutions carved into the wall.

From 480BC to 460BC, the Charioteer was sculpted. The method used to create the delicate features and the sturdy body was known as the wax method and involved the sculptor creating a clay design that he then covered in wax. As the molten bronze was added, the wax melted away and allowed the bronze to form over the clay and produce more detailed features. When it was discovered in 1896, two fragments of text were found near the statue, which hinted at the person who commissioned the bronze statue.

One text read, "Polyzalos dedicated me," which was found close to the statue. Polyzalos was an autocrat from the region of Sicily who was an accomplished chariot racer and won many races at the Pythian Games. The other text read that the sculptor who created the charioteer was probably Sotades. Historians believe that the statue was commissioned by Polyzalos to thank the gods for his triumphs, and that he favored the accomplished sculptor, Sotades.

480BC, the Persian forces attacked Delphi and threatened the sanctuary of the sacred site. They took control and overcame the Delphian forces.

458BC, a Spartan army marched on Delphi and restored the Dorian rule. Their armies captured three separate towns and drove the Persian armies from the area. The Spartans restored the natural leaders before Pericles, and his Athenian army marched on Delphi and restored Phocian rule in a conflict known as the Battle of Delphi.

373BC, a huge earthquake destroyed the temple of Apollo and caused huge landslides.

356BC, Delphi was undergoing restoration following the devastating damage caused by the earthquake when the 3rd Sacred War was fought. The conflict arose over an unpaid fine imposed by the Phocines on the Delphic forces for decimating sacred land and using treasure to fund their armies.

350BC, the theater at Delphi was constructed.

330BC, the 3rd Temple of Apollo was built. This temple was made from bronze and situated on Mount Parnassos.

279BC, Gauls attacked the sanctuary of Delphi led by Brennus the Galatian. His troops were reportedly defeated by the crumbling of stones from Mount Parnassus and a song from the Gods that deafened them.

191BC, the Romans tale control of Delphi. Although the site was revered by some of the Roman leaders, including Hadrian, most of their emperors pillaged it and took the treasures and artifacts back to Rome. While the site had been a famous and prestigious part of Greek history, the Romans had truly little regard for it, and it would seem the end was in sight for Delphi and the sanctuary it provided.

86BC, General Sulla funded his armies by sending his troops to Delphi to sack the temple of Apollo and return with the remaining treasures and monuments. The priests responsible for the temple's safety sent back reports that "*Apollo cries and weeps after his lost treasures every evening at his temple*," believing that the General would be afraid to bring the wrath of Apollo on his head. Sulla wasn't cowed by the statement and understood what the priests were trying to do. He sent back a message stating, "*Can't you see that Apollo is not weeping, but merely cheering upon the new glory of his gifts, seeing them travel to Rome, the Glorious city*." And with that statement, the era of the barbarian dawned.

48AD, the renaissance of Delhi was heralded and led by Hadrian, and interest in the sanctuary was renewed. The Emperor visited the site and paid homage to the temple of Apollo.

67AD, Emperor Nero competed in the Panhellenic games at Delphi.

98AD, Plutarch served the last thirty years of his life as a priest at Delphi. He was a Platonic Philosopher and a firm favorite of Hadrian, and during his time at Delphi, he wrote several works which mentioned the Oracle of Delphi and the importance of women in Greek society. He marveled at his contemporary; a lady called Arhiis, who was well versed in religious matters and was leading a movement dedicated to honoring Dionysus.

393AD, Emperor Theodosius ended all pagan games and worship in Greece. He decimated the remaining artifacts at the temple of Apollo. He took them to his capital city, Constantinople, while decreeing that the free exercise of Greek religion would cease from that time.

Following Roman rule and the cessation of Pagan worship, Delphi remained a town but lost any of its sacred ties. The age of the oracle was consigned to history, and although a brief return to the world's attention happened in 1436, it was destined to lie in waiting until the 17th century, when two European men would once again mention and catalog the area of Delphi.

The expedition of George Wheler and Jacob Spon would be considered groundbreaking, and the illustrations in their corresponding books showed the world a region filled with ruins and possible treasures. Still, it would be another two hundred years before the Great Excavation would uncover the majesty of Delphi and the hidden gems that lay beneath the surface.

Chapter 2:

Apollo and His Connection to Delphi

There is a Homeric Hymn to Apollo, which explains why the god chose the site of Delphi to make his home. He left his birthplace, the island of Delos, and made his way through the world, looking for the perfect place before he finally arrived at the magnificent Mount Parnassos. The area named Delphi consisted of a limestone rock that nestled beneath a broad fissure on the southern slope of the Mount and was topped by a pair of cliffs that shone with a glowing red light as the sun set in the evening.

The rock base was blessed with multiple springs and was accessed by a winding and narrow path that led to the oasis atop the dry and dusty slopes. The site must have been a welcoming shady retreat with its glades and fresh springs that create a magical area for the most powerful gods and the humblest humans. For Apollo, it seemed he had found his home, but there was a problem. The site was already dedicated to the goddess Gaia, the mother of the Earth. She resided in Delphi, guarded by her huge serpent named Python, and Apollo realized he would have to battle the beast to gain control of the sacred site. He shot the giant serpent with his tripod and left the corpse to rot, giving the site its alternate name of Python, which derived from the Greek word to rot.

Even though Apollo was a god, he was still governed by the laws of Zeus, and because he committed murder, he was sentenced to eight years working as a shepherd in the Greek province of Thessaly. His penance was fulfilled, and Apollo returned to Delphi to find his new home unguarded and in an array. Apollo now wondered who would be responsible for the administration of his new cult, and as he pondered, he spotted a boatload of Cretan sailors on their way to Pylo to fish. Apollo transformed himself into a dolphin and swam out to meet the boat. He jumped into the boat and terrified the Cretans, who then attempted to flip him out of the vessel, but the boat was in distress and in danger of sinking. Apollo called to Zeus to steer the boat to the coast of Crisa that lay just below Delphi to allow the crew to land on the beach, where he revealed himself in all his godly splendor to them.

Apollo spoke to them with wisdom and love and convinced them to leave their homeland and relocate to Delphi to serve as his priests. The story is given credence by the discovery of Cretan figurines and models dating from 800BC. Some of the figures are in the style of Daedalus, the master craftsman of Crete at that time.

Back at Delphi, Gaia still resided, and even as a dispossessed goddess, she was still revered and continued attracting worshippers to the site. The sanctuary still had a large number of female priestesses, and this empowered the status of the earth goddess and her followers. Her daughter, Thesis, lived on the island with the mighty sea god Poseidon. Thesis was the daughter of Gaia and Hydro, although some accounts name her as the mother of Gaia, who created the eternal mud that the earth sprung from.

Dionysus

Another interesting aspect of the newly formed cult was the god Dionysus who shared Delphi with his brother Apollo and became the main deity in the winter months when Apollo sought warmer climes. While Apollo visited Hyperborean in the north and reveled in the country of eternal youth and the presence of everlasting beauty where disease and aging didn't exist, Dionysus ruled the sanctuary at Delphi and brought his unique style to the land.

The Rites of Dionysus

Ancient artwork and tales from the era depict the rites of Dionysus as hedonistic and sexually charged rituals of wine and music that offered the participants the opportunity to return to nature. This god is often portrayed as a raging bull or a leopard, and he invited everybody to participate in his rituals. All were equal, including enslaved people, criminals, and non-citizens. The rituals involved the use of wine to intoxicate the participants and give them the sensation of being filled with the essence of God as they played the role of the maenads, also known as the "raving ones." These figures would then dress in wild animal skins and partake of poppy seeds while they worked themselves into a frenzy with drinking and dancing.

Following the drinking, they would roam through the hillsides holding aloft a long stick covered in vine leaves while wearing a wreath of ivy on their head. The rites included hunting wild animals and feasting on their flesh, followed by wild orgiastic sex with members abandoning all their moral codes and becoming part of the wild. Dionysus and his rites couldn't have been more contrasting to the calm and rational cult of his brother Apollo. It was understood that as Apollo left, Delphi Dionysus would perform his rites to mark a seasonal death and rebirth theme that cleared the sacred site of negativity and suppressed energy, ready for the return of Apollo and the oracle.

Apollo and His Complicated Love Life

Apollo had many love affairs, including male and female lovers, and produced multiple offspring within these unions. Here are some of his more celebrated partners and their influence on his story:

Daphne

She was a nymph who was desperate to escape Apollo's advances, and, in an attempt to evade him, she turned herself into a laurel tree. Gaia heard her cries for help and replaced her form with a natural laurel tree. Because of this fact, the leaves of the laurel tree have been used to represent Apollo and became the symbol of victory in the Pythian Games.

The Muses

Apollo had affairs with all nine of the Muses and was enamored of them all. He couldn't choose who to marry, and so he remained unwed but produced four children from his conquests.

Rhoeo

A princess of the island Naxos, she bore Apollo a son called Anius, whom he raised and educated because he was so in love with her. He also made her sisters into goddesses and introduced them into the godly world.

Coronis

The daughter of the King of Lapiths was much loved by Apollo. When she fell pregnant with what he believed to be his child, he learned that she had betrayed him and slept with another god. Apollo brought his wrath to her door when he sent his sister Artemis to remove the baby from her stomach, and he then gave the infant to the wisest of all the centaurs Chiron to raise as his own child.

Hecuba

The wife of the king of Troy, Hecuba, bore Apollo a son named Troilus who was the subject of a prophecy by Pythia who declared that the Coty of Troy wouldn't fall to its enemies providing Troilus reached the age of twenty-one. He was captured and killed by Achilles, the hero of the Trojan wars, which brought about the fall of Troy. Apollo avenged the death of his son by slaying Achilles and returned his distraught mother to the Anatolian state of Lycia so she could live out the rest of her life in peace.

Male Lovers

Adonis

The mortal lover of Aphrodite, Adonis, was changed into a female form so he could become the lover of Apollo.

Helenus

A gentle and intelligent seer Helenus was the twin brother of Cassandra and a beloved lover of Apollo, who gifted his lover an ivory bow. Later in their relationship, Helenus used the same bow to wound his former lover on his hand.

Branchus

A mortal shepherd came across the god in the woods as he herded sheep. The shepherd was so overcome with Apollo's beauty that he kissed him. Apollo responded in kind, and the two became lovers. As a reward for his love Apollo bestowed the power of prophecy on Branchus and his descendants, who then became the Branchides, a powerful tribe of prophets and soothsayers.

Admetus

During his exile for the murder of the Python, Apollo was given the job of serving as a herdsman to the king of Pherae, named Admetus. It is written that although the god was a mighty force, he remained as a servant to serve Admetus because of the overwhelming love he felt for the king. Apollo regularly served cheese and wine to his lover, which embarrassed his family and brought forward a decree that he must be killed. Admetus escaped his death by marrying a princess called Alcestis. Apollo sealed the union by providing them with a wedding chariot pulled by animals he had tamed and sealed the couple's fate.

Hyacinth

A beautiful athletic Spartan prince Hyacinth was a firm favorite of Apollo. The pair would often play games and exercise together. When they were out in a field throwing discus one day, the breeze caused by a jealous wind god blew the discus off course. It struck Hyacinth in the head and killed him immediately. Apollo was so grief-struck that he created a flower from the drops of blood that fell from his lover's head. There is still a festival of Hyacinth held to remember the death of the prince and celebrate his resurrection and ascent to heaven.

Apollo and His Attributes and Symbols

Apollo was the god of colonization and gave his advice on colonization via his oracle that encouraged the foundation of the city of Troy and other colonies during the period around 600BC and before. He was also regarded as the god of reason and order, the total opposite of his brother Dionysus but this was a positive aspect of their relationship according to ancient Greek reasoning. They believed that the two types of personality were complementary and that when Apollo left Delphi, the energy that Dionysus brought was cleansing and much needed.

He was symbolized by a bow and arrow but was also pictured with a kithara, a more complicated version of the lyre. He was also depicted as a handsome beardless youth who is often reclining against a tree with an air of calm and beauty. He was the epitome of youth and beauty and is normally represented by a large-eyed stare with his head tilted and his soft curls grazing the nape of his neck. His body is the divine form of nakedness which, in later sculptures, was cloaked with a cape to mark his modesty in the later Empire. Some representations also include a halo that predates the Christian use of the corona.

Apollo was a much-loved god and represented all positive aspects of humanity, like poetry, purification, healing, light, knowledge, and music. He became known as the dutiful son of the god Zeus and even when he did defy his father, he accepted his punishments and banishments with grace. He was attributed with a darker side as the bringer of the plague and the god of divine retribution, but he took these duties seriously. He took part in many mythical contests with his musical counterparts Pan and Marsaya until he was declared the undisputed master of music by King Midas. The latter judged his lyre music to be preferable to the more chaotic flute music of his competitors.

Apollo is all around the site at Delphi, and visitors can't help but feel his influence at every turn. Today we know that Greek mythology is part of history and no more than a series of fantastic tales, but at Delphi, that changes, and you can almost hear his voice on the wind as he revisits his favorite place on Earth.

Chapter 3:

The Oracle of Delphi

The word oracle comes from the Latin verb "to speak," and we commonly use terms from the same verb as oral, orate, and oration. Oracle, however, has a more defined meaning, especially when applied to Greek mythology, and it refers to the priest or priestess that is used to convey the predictions of the gods to humans. They are the medium chosen to be the god's representative on Earth and are required to fill certain criteria.

There were multiple sites in Ancient Greece that were deemed to be sanctuaries, and some of them also offered oracles for consultation. The god Zeus had important oracles at Olympia and Dodona, while Apollo spoke through oracles as far as Asia and throughout Greece. Delphi was the most enduring and well-known of all the oracles and sanctuaries. Delphi held a special place in people's lives for millennia and has appeared in texts and artwork throughout history. The location of the site and the reference to it as the "navel of the world" have made it a sacred site for pilgrims and worshippers to visit for eons.

Delphi has an otherworldly feel as it sits on a rocky plateau beneath the magnificent Mount Parnassus, and it truly feels like the land of the gods rather than a site for human occupation. However, its rise in importance was mainly due to its position on an important trade route between Corinth and Northern Greece, which meant it became more accessible to visitors. Its status as a sanctuary appealed to visitors from the larger, more important cities like Sparta and Athens and its popularity and importance increased as a result.

The Oracle

Although there is extraordinarily little known about these women who served as the oracle in Delphi, they were known as the Pythia. Once chosen, they would serve for life. They would live at the sanctuary for the rest of their lives, and, in some cases, there was more than one Pythia serving due to the demand for their services. At one stage, three

Pythia were appointed to serve the sanctuary at the height of its popularity.

What Did They Do?

As the term oracle suggests, they conveyed the word of the gods, in this case, Apollo, to the people. In today's career world, they would be given the title of "head of the knowledge economy." They would be responsible for the cultivation of information and serve as the advisor for all matters, trivial and non-trivial, when called upon to do so.

She was called upon to give her advice about matters of state, religious concerns, warfare, intercity connections, and the foundation of new cultures. She would also be asked about matters of the heart, love, childbirth, and how to fall pregnant. This wasn't just a demanding job but a position that could influence society and change the course of history. The fact that this position would always be awarded to a woman of good breeding must have irked some of the Greek males. This was a patriarchal and paternalistic society where women didn't occupy higher positions and were more likely to be found in the home raising their families.

Some accounts of the Pythia have alluded to this fact by suggesting the oracle would babble unintelligible nonsense that would then be interpreted by the attending male priests who were, in fact, the true link to the gods. Although there are conflicting accounts, most sources suggest that the Pythia was the sole purveyor of these prophecies, and the only male influences were in lowly roles serving her every need.

How Did the Consultation Process Evolve?

Imagine if the oracle sat daily and gave consultations on the hour. It would hardly feel special to gain access and be part of the process. The exclusivity of the consultation needed to be preserved, and this meant restricting the times the oracle was available. During three of the winter months, the oracle retired and was unavailable for a consult because the god Apollo would have sought warmer climes during the colder part of the year. During the remaining nine months of the year, the Pythia would sit for just one day per month, which meant there were just nine days when she was available.

Even on these designated days, the process wasn't always guaranteed to take place. A goat was taken to the sacred site, and freezing water was sprinkled on it. If the goat shivered, the oracle would receive visitors. They would have to wait until the following month if it didn't. Once it had been established that the consultants would be granted an audience, the process began to vet visitors before they met with the Pythia. Each member would have to pay a fee and offer a sacrificial sweet offering called a pelanos before they were led to a natural spring to bathe and purify themselves.

Next, they formed a queue according to their importance. Delphians headed the line, followed by people who had connections to the sanctuary. They were followed by other Greek residents, while non-Greeks were admitted last. A further sacrifice would be made to the gods of the heavens and the Pythia before the consultations began. The Pythia would have already bathed in the sacred spring and made her own offering to Apollo by burning laurel leaves.

Reports about what happened next vary. Some say she sat on a tripod in the center of the consultation room, while other reports say she sat in a chasm in the floor. Wherever she sat matters not, although some historians believe the chasm was the source of gases that may have been inhaled by the Pythia, leading to a trance-like state. She may or may not have been drugged, but when the consultee entered the room and asked their questions, they honestly believed the answers came directly from their beloved god Apollo.

While the consultees may have been there on personal business, others would be there to represent states and cities. The oracle of Delphi was a competent law and order source, and she is credited with the rise of democracy and the growth of Greece during the sixth century BC. Her advice about disputes and growth meant that she fulfilled a key role and became a power player in the ancient Greek world.

Interpreting the Words of the Oracle

Scholars and priests are known to have worked with the Pythia to interpret her words for the mortals who attended her consults. How the responses were recorded is unknown. Some historians believe they were written in hexameter poetry, and others believe they were uttered in riddle format. However, the lack of historical evidence means none of these theories can be proven, but there are stories about the ambiguity of her answers and the openness to misinterpretation. She was also the speaker of truths and never shied away from telling an unwelcome truth to even the most important visitors to her shrine.

In one report, a Spartan man consulted with the Pythia and expected to be confirmed as the wisest man in Greece. The oracle replied with a list of men who were considered wiser despite his protests. A representative from Megara, a historic city in West Attica, once visited the oracle to confirm that Megara was the best city in Greece. The Pythia named two cities that were better than Megara and then stated that it didn't even qualify as third or fourth. She asked why the Megarian didn't see that coming.

It seems that Pythia wasn't averse to a sharp-tongued reply, no matter the status of the person asking the question. Although the responses came from Apollo, she was also considered beyond reproach and unimpeachable. Other scholars and augurs of the time were criticized heavily, while Pythia and her utterings were beyond reproach, and she remained the voice of truth to all Greeks.

It is known that many tried to manipulate Pythia with trickery and bribes, but she remained steadfast in her honesty. She was the pantheon of virtue, and she led the campaign to free Athens and the whole of Greece from tyranny and the forces who would try and capture the nation. If she believed the question that she was asked was unreasonable or had been subject to manipulation, she would refuse to answer even when the fee had been paid. The gods protected her role, and she was always guided by their power.

Who Could Become a Pythia?

Ancient texts are unfortunately silent on this subject. The author William Golding wrote a novel named "The Double Tongue" about a local Greek girl who failed to find a suitable husband and decided to dedicate herself to the role of Pythia instead, but that's fiction and kind of downplays the importance and standing the role involved. More likely, the Pythia would be an older woman who had lived a good life and found herself as a respected member of the community who was a good listener and communicator. According to the only written reports from the time of the Pythia, which came from Plutarch in the first century AD, the questions were surprisingly mundane. Will I win? Should I travel? Is marriage right for me? Does it seem that straightforward questions were put to the Pythia? Was it different in the ancient time of the sixth century BC? Probably. There were more weighty matters to consider, and the Pythia would no doubt have been asked more complicated and influential questions.

Some of the More Momentous Consultations with the Pythia

The most famous consultation must have been when the King of Lydia asked the oracle if he should attack his enemy Cyrus the Great of Persia. He was told his attack would signal the end of a great empire, which he interpreted to mean he would be successful, and he went ahead with the attack. His defeat signaled the end of his empire, so the oracle was correct. She just failed to tell him it would be his own empire that would be defeated.

Julian the Apostate

Julian was a heathen and Hellenic believer who strongly opposed Christianity and believed in the prophetic powers of the Pythia. He believed that his pagan and philosophical approach would allow his rule as Emperor from 331AD to 363Ad to bring together the two beliefs of the ancient Greeks and the more modern Christians. He sent his trusted envoy and physician to consult the Pythia in 362AD to determine if he could be successful with his plan.

The oracle predicted his demise and the end of the oracle in the same prediction. She told him to tell the king that Phoebus (an epithet of Apollo when he was connected to the sun) was no more, and there would be no more prophecy. She told of the loss of a talking laurel or fountain and proclaimed that the marsh water would also be mute. Her prophecy told of the rich courts being torn down and all being lost.

Just twenty months later, Julian was struck down and killed by a spear to the back while fighting in the Persian wars. His consultation proved to be the final recorded prophecy by the oracle and signaled the end of pagan worship in Greece.

Philip of Macedonia

During the third holy war, Philip II was eager to make his position in Macedonia stronger, and he consulted with the oracle to ask for help to consolidate his control. She told him to fight his battles with silver spears, and he would be assured of victories. Philip realized that her answer contained a reference to the silver coins he had just minted rather than actual silver spears. He concentrated on becoming more financially powerful and acquired several gold and silver mines which consolidated his position and his control.

King Grinos

Greek commercial and religious ties had been expanding and had encompassed a colony in North Africa known as Thera, which was ruled by King Grinos. He consulted the oracle to help him solve the problems he was encountering on his island and was told he should colonize Libya and benefit from the resources there. Grinos decided to ignore the word of Apollo and declared himself too old for such adventures. This led to the wrath of the gods falling on his kingdom, and the island of Thera underwent a seven-year drought.

Grinos returned to the oracle to ask for their help to end the drought and was reminded that Apollo had already answered his question and the solution remained in his grasp. Grinos then returned to his homeland, amassed an army, and began his mission to conquer Libya and bring prosperity to the combined nations.

Homer

The legendary author and influential thinker of the time, Homer was on a mission to find out information about his parents and where he had been born. He consulted the oracle and was told that his birthplace was the island of Ios that would receive him when he died, but he must beware of the riddles of little children. Despite the fatality of the prediction, Homer couldn't resist visiting the island of Ios, and when he arrived, he was greeted by a group of children fishing on the shore.

He asked them what they were fishing for and was told, "What we catch, we leave. What we do not catch, we bring back." Homer was completely baffled by the riddle and swiftly reminded of Pythia's prophecy. Horrified, he fled the area and slipped on the muddy road that led from the seashore. He hit his head and died immediately.

For reference's sake, the children spoke of head lice and the fact that those who found their lice killed them and those who didn't, carried them away on their heads.

Other versions of the death of Homer report that he was so grief-stricken by his inability to solve the riddle that he died from his grief. Another tells a tale that Homer became ill and returned to the island to fulfill the prophecy. As with many of the oracle tales, there are different interpretations and stories based on her prophecies and power.

Chapter 4:

The Great Excavation

In the early 20th century, archaeology was still in its developmental stage, with any treasure or finds designated to appear in the museums of the US or Europe. The methods they used weren't what we would call ethical today, and the teams of archaeologists were driven by costs and time pressure. They were funded by individuals or groups who expected them to deliver the finds in record time and for lower costs to make their work profitable.

This meant that some excavations were rushed, and early archaeological digs used dynamite and other destructive materials to access the sites. Light organic materials and the methods used to remove them meant that seeds and pollens from the area were destroyed. There were also many backroom deals between the local leaders and the archaeologists on site, meaning that various objects ended up in certain museums based on who could pay the biggest bribe.

Perhaps the most famous excavation of the time was when the wealthy Lord Carnarvon hired Howard Carter to dig in Egypt and find something special for him. Carter was an experienced archaeologist with ten years of working with Sir Petrie, an accomplished expert in the field, and he brought a wealth of experience to the team.

Carter was working in Egypt when the First World War was raging through Europe, and he felt that his lack of supplies and success hampered him. He agreed with Carnarvon that if he hadn't discovered something by the year 1922, the dig would finish, and he would return to the UK. In November 1922, a telegram was sent to Carnarvon, which stated, "At last... I have made a wonderful discovery, a magnificent tomb with the seals intact ... recovered, and waiting for your arrival."

The discovery became a milestone for archaeology and created a media frenzy about history. The pair staged a spectacular tomb opening ceremony filmed by the media in which they broke the seals, shone a light into the tomb, and described all the marvelous things they could see. Most people believe they had already broken the seals the day before and resealed them just to satisfy the media frenzy the find had attracted. Carnarvon may have been driven by the desire to add spectacular objects to his personal collection. Still, for the archaeological community, it showed that real information could be obtained from undisturbed tombs, which meant a new era for their digs. Hopefully, tomb-robbing and looting would become a thing of the past.

Greek Excavations

Back in Greece, a man named Sir Arthur Evans had moved to the site of Knossos in Crete in 1895 following the death of his wife. He collaborated with a respected archaeologist David Hogarth, and the pair began their excavations in 1900. They discovered evidence of the Minoan people and their existence on Crete from around 7,000BC to 6500BC, which more modern carbon dating methods have confirmed since. The evidence he found included pottery, burial art, friezes, and a palace that had been partially destroyed. The most important finds at the site were two tablets named Linear A and Linear B, which contained syllabic script and ideograms that predated the Greek alphabet by centuries. The language is called Mycenean Greek, and only one of the tablets has since been translated.

The Great Excavation

Visitors to Greece had often stopped at the site of Delphi and considered what hidden treasure lay beneath the surface of the village renamed Kastri. It was well recorded that the area had been pillaged and sacked by a myriad of cultures, including rulers like Nero, Constantine the Great, and the Phocians, all through the existence of the sacred site. All that remained was a series of ruins that merely hinted at what lay beneath the surface of the speckled earth.

A French archaeologist were assigned to discover what was there and bring to light the story of Delphi and its fascinating past. In the 19th century, work began around the wall that enclosed the site. Still, the villagers who lived in Kastri weren't enthusiastic at the prospect of a bunch of foreigners seeking to relocate the whole village so it could be dismantled. Fate stepped in and stopped work with another earthquake at the site, which meant the excavations were abandoned until further notice.

Five years after the earthquake, the Greek State leader, who was a forward-thinking man named Trikoupis, recognized that foreign aid was needed to help any further work in the Delphi area, and he made a deal with the French Government for preliminary work to start at the site under the leadership of an archaeologist called B. Haussoulier.

Across the Atlantic, interest was piqued in America, especially in New York and Boston, where a group of men was eager to discover new digs in the ancient world. They began to campaign for funds to challenge the French and win the rights to carry out excavations in Delphi. Despite their enthusiasm and passion for the project, they faced stiff opposition from the French, who had men in Greece and a sizeable budget provided by their backers. The Americans simply didn't have the negotiators or the funds in place, so the Greek Parliament passed an act to give the agreement to expropriate Delphi to the French.

The excavations began in 1892 with the removal of the whole village of Kastri and the four hundred dwellings which housed over a thousand people. The team built a mini railway to clear the rubble and take earth away as they began uncovering the buildings below the surface. Over four hundred men, miles of rail track, and seventy-five individual cars covered the site, extending to over a mile and a half. Work continued until the team found virgin soil and an assemblage of artistic wonders.

The area revealed votive buildings, the polygonal wall which circled the site, and the theater, stadium, and in the center, the temple of Apollo. The following year the site was further excavated to reveal the Sacred Way, Sibyls Rock, the sanctuary of Athena, and assorted statues and treasures. Perhaps the most thrilling part of the excavation was the uncovering of various treasuries, which all housed the treasure brought by individuals from allotted cities to the temple to show their allegiance and love for the god Apollo. Outside the walls, they discovered a Merchant's Portico, the ancient version of a gift shop where merchants would sell various objects presumably related to the religion of the god Apollo.

The archaeological museum at Delphi has a detailed and chronological display of the treasures which were found at the site during the Great Excavation and after. Details of the museum can be found later in the book, with a floor-to-floor list of the objects displayed. Around Delphi, other museums house interesting exhibits and are a must-see if you visit the site.

The Sanctuary of Apollo

Although it isn't classed as an official museum, the whole Sanctuary of Apollo is a dedicated historical site that will take your breath away the second you see it. The South section, the West section, and the entry to the Sanctuary all house a myriad of treasures that are accessible to visitors.

The central part of the sanctuary is dominated by the Sacred Way, which rises to finish in the central complex masterpiece, the Temple of Apollo. Take the path which was trodden by pilgrims for millennia aiming to find the guidance and sanctuary of the god Apollo while you pass the several stone pedestals that line your way.

Observe the Bull of Kerkyra that traveled from Corfu to grace the Sanctuary and wonder at the remains of the Spartan monument that was dedicated to their beloved leader Lysander. A few steps later, you will see the small conical stone representing the site's claim to be the "navel of the world."

Taking the northern path leads you past the Athenian treasury, the most magnificent of the individual treasuries and home to the remaining portion of a column that once supported the Sphynx of Naxos. Discover the Rock of Sybil, which was once the site of the earliest Pythia and marks where she would consult with her attendants. Take time to examine the wall, which was once the base of the second temple of Apollo, and discover the minute inscriptions covering it.

The Temple of Apollo dominates the Sanctuary, and you can marvel at the majesty of the building that once housed the eternal flame and played host to countless pilgrims who stood in the open air and worshipped the might Apollo and learned from the Delphic Maxims that decorated the corridor to the entrance.

Take the eastern path to the site of the Serpentine Column, which was reproduced in 2015 to mark the spot where the original bronze column stood that celebrates the Greek forces that defeated the Persians at the Battle of Plataea in the fifth century BC. The original column can now be seen in Istanbul, where it stands after it had been sacked by Constantine the Great during his time in Delphi.

Rising in a magnificent form above the temple is the Pythian Theater, the home of the celebrated plays staged there every four years and named the Pythian Festival. They attracted thousands of visitors and were some of the most popular plays of the time. The climb to the top is time-consuming but well worth the effort. The views of the Sanctuary and the surrounding countryside are magnificent and breathtaking.

Return to the Sanctuary and seek the eastern path to the Castalian Spring, where the visitors and the oracle would bathe to cleanse themselves before they visited the Pythia and consulted her.

The Galaxidi Museum

Although the museum isn't as ancient as the Delphi site, this Naval and Historical Museum is still worth a visit. It houses artifacts relating to all things marine and includes a collection of objects relating to local boats, ships, accessories, and nautical objects from the area of Galaxidi. There is an art gallery containing paintings relating to Greek shipping and a collection of exhibits garnered from the boatyards of the region. Many of the objects were donated by local people and included a fascinating array of charts, compasses, barometers, hooks, and other minutiae from the naval world.

In 2007, the museum acquired the Argonaut collection of stamps which are documents relating to the history of shipping from antiquity to the present day. There are commemoration stamps from the Battle of St. Lucia and other memorable sea battles. There are stamps from history that depict famous men from history, including Winston Churchill and other august individuals.

Chrisso Folk Museum

Just 4km from Delphi, this quirky folk museum is home to an array of costumes from the region dating back over four hundred years. If you long for a change of focus and a more decorative type of exhibit, this is the place to visit. Examine the costumes and accessories which cover the whole floor of the museum and marvel at the delicacy of the lace work that was manufactured in the area. It is a fascinating look at the different styles of costumes worn by Greek throughout the ages and allows you to see firsthand the mastery that went into their creations.

The British Military Cemetery

Traveling from Amfissa to Lamia, just beyond the village of Gravia, you may spot a sign that seems out of place. There is a solid stone wall with a small sign that reads "The BRALO BRITISH CEMETERY," and this marks the site of a well-kept yet very British monument. It was built in 1917 to house the graves of men from the Commonwealth who died in the war defending the Bralos area against the enemy and protecting them from the German submarines which were active in the Med at the time.

The cemetery was used for two years and had a hundred and two graves belonging to men born in the Commonwealth and who died in the war or because of the Spanish flu that ravaged the world from 1918 until 1920. The site is open daily and can be visited whenever you like, and the route from Delphi takes just fifty minutes by car.

Chapter 5:

The Archaeological Museum of Delphi

I n 1903, it soon became clear that the discoveries that had emerged due to the French archaeological campaign La Grande Fouille or the Great Excavation would need a more permanent home and a place where visitors could see them. The operation had already involved various nationalities and excavations by multiple archeological crews unearthing a cornucopia of finds. The village of Kastri was now transformed into a thriving community filled with technical teams dedicated to removing debris and renovating old houses to become homes for the people who were participating in the Great Excavation.

The next natural step was the inauguration of a museum which happened in 1903 and was funded by Andreas Syngros and designed by Albert Tournaire. The museum was designed to display a collection depending on their contextual sites, and the principal monuments were reproduced in plaster. The idea was to give visitors access to the discoveries in a simple and self-explanatory way, but it lacked any chronological or historical arrangement.

The number of visitors to the site grew, and the space soon became restricted. It was filled with exhibits, and they occupied every inch of the museum, which meant the visitors found it cramped and had difficulty appreciating the antiquities. The museum was a resounding success with both domestic and international visitors, and feedback about the plaster recreations of the monuments deemed that it was "too French," and more Greek influences were called for.

In 1935, the original museum was closed, and the construction of a new building was commissioned. The plans differed greatly from the original museum and concentrated more on displaying the antiquities in chronological order with extensive labeling and cataloging. The museum needed a more professional feel as the artifacts became more significant and needed to be represented by the trends of the time. Archaeology had become a significant part of the culture at that time, and the new museum was designed to be part of this new vision.

The museum was completed in 1939, and the antiquities were in place, ready for a new wave of visitors, but the rest of the world had different ideas. As the world prepared to go to war, it was decided that the antiquities needed to be moved to keep them safe. Fortunately, during their time in Delphi, the Romans had already dug extensive tombs. They were used along with specially constructed vaults to store some of the less valuable and bulkier objects. The more precious exhibits were transported to Athens to be stored at the Bank of Greece in secure vaults until it was deemed to be safe to return them to Delphi.

Even though the war finished in 1945, it had already been decided that the museum would not reopen until 1952 as Delphi was in the heart of the combat zone relating to the Greek Civil War which was raging at the time. In the meantime, some of the more important items could be seen on display in the Museum of Athens until they could be returned to their original home.

Between 1952 and 1958, visitors returned in their droves to the museum to see the newly arranged artifacts, but it soon became clear that the museum's vision in 1939 was not working in the late 1950s. A new renovation was needed to bring the museum into the second half of the twentieth century. This time, the project was overseen by a completely Greek team consisting of architect Patroklos Karantinos and the renowned archaeologist and director of the museum, Christos Karouzos, who was sequestered from the Museum of Athens to work with the exhibits he had looked after for years. The whole project was supervised by the ephor of antiquities, Ioanna Konstantinou.

The third phase of the museum's development finally opened its doors to the public in 1961. The museum quickly became one of the most visited sites in Greece and profited from the economic and cultural renaissance of the area that brought tourists to the site from all parts of the world. Greece was undergoing regeneration and was concentrating on its rich history and culture to attract new interest to Greek shores.

The architect Karantinos constructed two new halls for the exhibits, which allowed a flood of natural light to flow through the exhibition and highlighted his interest in Greek Modernism. He worked with Karouzos to place the exhibits in a less structured way that concentrated on sculpture. The process highlighted the features and natural beauty of the statues but removed some of the architectural contexts. The compromise works well and allows visitors to see the exhibits in their best position and under the optimum circumstances.

The museum grew in popularity in the following decades and, by 1998, it was regularly attracting over 300 000 visitors annually, which was only surpassed by the Museum of Athens. It was no surprise to anybody that the sixties style of the building needed to be further renovated, and between 1999 and 2003, the Greek architect Alexandros Tombazis was tasked with the new design. He is considered one of the leading Greek architects today and, in 1999, was a leading light in the field of Metabolist architecture at the time. He designed multiple projects before his Delphi commission, and his contemporary style became a major design factor in the new museum.

The façade of the building is sleek and modern and designed to facilitate the numerous visitors and make their visit as effortless and interesting as possible. The new design included a large lobby, a modern and efficiently styled eatery, and a gift shop. While the collection underwent a transformation and became more effective, a new section was created to present the theories and development of archaeology and scholarships related to history.

The museum isn't the biggest attraction but is an integral part of the Delphi experience. It contains a rich collection of hundreds of exhibits which range from marble statues to humble coins, which unfold over two floors to give the visitor an impressive snapshot of time in Greek history. Most of the attractions are available to touch and include fascinating details of the period. The Charioteer is situated in the last room, providing an impressive climax to the tour and leaving the visitor with a sense of wonder and grace. There is also a miniature reproduction of the whole site of Delphi that explains how the temples and oracles were affected by elements, including war, earthquakes, and rockslides until it developed into a mountainside.

The Fourteen Rooms and What They Contain

Rooms 1 and 2

These two rooms contain the most ancient exhibits in the museum, including items from the Bronze Age. In Greece, there was a settlement known as Mycenae, where the residents formed clay figures and rough examples of furniture decorated with mythical creatures. Many of the exhibits are bronze votive objects, and the rooms also contain figures of warriors from the Geometric era.

Room 3

This room is dominated by the archaic form of art, which dates to the period between 800BC and 480BC and follows the Greek Dark Age. It contains the two statues of Cleobis and Biton, who were two brothers featured in the tales from Argos. The room also houses square sections from the Treasury of the Sicyonians, which is part of the sanctuary of

Apollo; the stones depict scenes from the Argonaut expedition and tell the story of Greek heroes like Zeus, who captured Europe while maintaining the form of a bull. Other bronze tiles show depictions of Hercules and Ulysses in action with decorative motifs around the edge.

Room 4

This room is the first indication of the treasures that lie ahead and contains the relics found in an area of Delphi named the Sacred Way. There are various objects of sculpture known as the chryselephantine form, which means they have been overlaid with gold and ivory. The room holds three separate sculptures that represent the Apollonian triad.

Room 5

Containing the Sphinx of Naxos and elegant female figures that were extracted from another treasury on the Sacred Way. The room is decorated with friezes depicting the Trojan War, the siege of Troy, the race of people known as the Giants, and the Judgement of Paris, which was one of the events that led to the Trojan War.

The room is completely dominated by the Sphinx, which towers above the other exhibits on an impressive column in the center of the room. The column, the capital, and the statue total a huge twelve meters in height. The original statue was sited at the Halos, a space close to the Temple of Apollo and the location of ancient rituals and gatherings.

Room 6

This room is dedicated to the façade of the Temple of Apollo and is filled with impressive statues and sculptures from the archaic and classic periods of art from that era. The sculptures in this room are attributed to Antenor, a prominent sculptor of the time, but may also have been carved by Praxias. Three male and three female figures line the entrance and flan a carriage driven by four horses and carrying the God Apollo. It is thought to represent the arrival of Apollo at Delphi for the first time and is believed to date back to 850BC. Nike is also featured in a running position with her knee raised and surrounded by Sphinxes.

Room 7

This area is dedicated to the Treasury of the Athenians and contains the items brought to Delphi by early Athenians who worshipped at the temple of Apollo. They brought offerings and asked for the blessings of the gods to be bestowed on their houses. The room is filled with carved depictions of famous scenes from Greek history involving Athena, Theseus, and the killing of the Minotaur and the bull of Marathon. One change in style is the triptych telling of the twelve labors of Hercules in chronicle order which includes the slaying of the Hydra and capturing the Erymanthian boar.

Room 8

This room contains some of the first pottery items in the museum, including a shallow bowl decorated with an unusual depiction of the god Apollo playing a lire with a blackbird in the foreground. The plate was found in a grave that was underneath the museum. It also contains remnants of the Delphic Hymns, which are thought to have been written around the 130BC era and were believed to have been written for a performance two years later. The

Delphic Hymns are the first notated form of music from the Western world with the composer's name attached to them.

Room 9

Items in this room are from one of the temples that formed the Sanctuary of Athena Pronaia, which included the Tholos of Delphi. They consist of a central case with three stunning figures in bronze of running females attributed to the goddess Athena. Another case contains three naked male figures, one playing a lute and the other two running between the attic workshops. There is another bronze figure of a female holding a cauldron which was used to burn incense in the temple.

Room 10

In this room, you can find actual architectural objects from the temple with stone carved lion heads and statues of women dressed in swirling peplos, a body-length garment worn by Greek women from the 5th century BC until the Hellenistic period, which began in 300BC. The sculptures were found in the earliest Asclepiad healing temples dedicated to Asclepius, the first medical-related demigod in Greek mythology. His skills were so powerful that it was written that he could raise the dead, and pilgrims would travel long distances just to visit his temple and ask for his healing powers to be bestowed on them.

Room 11

Containing relics from the period of 336BC to 280BC, the most important exhibit is the Dancers of Delphi and the ex voto of Daochos. The Daochos relic is a long marble base with nine sections for statues that represent the members of his family, including Apollo, Anconeus with his three sons, and other prominent historical figures.

The Dancers of Delphi is an elaborate column with delicately carved foliage at the base from which a trio of dancers emerges holding their hands aloft. It is believed they held a tripod at one time, but it was damaged over time and removed from the statue. There are also two statues of elderly men wearing traditional Greek garments from the age known as a himation. One of the figures wears his gown with his right shoulder and chest bare, indicating he was an Apollo priest from the year 280BC.

Room 12

In this room, the first artifacts from the Roman era appear, including the statue of Antinous. This Greek youth was the favorite and probable lover of the emperor Hadrian. There is a bust of the Roman general who was responsible for the conquer of Delphi in 198BC and heralded a length of Roman rule. Theatrical frieze parts adorn the south side of the room and once again celebrate the labors of Hercules but with a Roman twist in their decoration.

Room 13

The room of the Charioteer. The classic bronze statue was found in 1896 at the Sanctuary of Apollo and is a representation of a chariot driver from the time. Most bronze statues from the era were melted down or repurposed, but the Charioteer survived because it was buried under a rock fall caused by the earthquake in 373BC. The young man is strictly symmetrical but appears to be overtly human, and his painted eyes inlaid with precious stones are eerily natural.

Room 14

This room is the final room of the floor and represents the final years of the sanctuary before it fell quiet. Three marble heads represent figures from the 1st century AD until the 4th century AD. They are believed to have been of priests or philosophers from the age, including Plutarch, the author of celebrated biographies of both Roman and Greek luminaries.

The ground floor is a large exhibition space containing more eclectic items dating from Late Antiquity to classical.

The whole experience is intense and should take no more than ninety minutes to fully explore.

Chapter 6:

The Delphic Maxims

Most people have heard about the Ten Commandments in the Christian church and what they represent but few people are aware of the Delphic Maxims and where they originate from. The Maxims are a collection of 147 written edicts that were redesigned to help you live a good life and a worthy way of living. They are believed to have been written by a group of men known as the Seven Sages, who visited the oracle at Delphi and became inspired by the messages they received from Apollo and by his wisdom. They didn't set out to write a list of rules or absolutes to follow; they are just a framework to follow to lead your best life.

The Seven Sages lived in the early sixth century BC and were a mixed bag of philosophers and other important public figures who were highly regarded at that time. They are usually referenced as the following:

- Thales of Miletus created the first system of natural philosophy. It was the first known man to attempt to explain the physical form of the world that had only ever been explained in mythical and spiritual terms.

- Chilon of Sparta is credited with being the first Spartan to militarize their famous armies. He was an intelligent and humorous man who believed that brevity was the root of all philosophy, while others expounded long-winded philosophical statements. He is credited with many Greek proverbs and portions of the Delphic Maxims that are still relevant today. In an inscription at a Greek bath in Ostia, it is claimed that "Cunning Chilon taught to fart in silence."

- Solon of Athens was the author of the laws that shaped democracy in the legendary city of Athens.

- Bias of Priene, a sage man who was a Master of Advocacy and a prolific poet who wrote a 2,000-line poem about the island Iona and how to make it more prosperous.

- Cleoboulus of Lindus was a renowned poet and leader of the Lindians. He was referred to as a tyrant, but this meant he was a strong leader yet fair. His rules lasted over forty years, and today his tomb is a well-visited site for tourists.

- Pittacus of Mitylene governed the province on the island of Lesbos. It was instrumental in taking power from the higher-born members of society and allowing the working and popular classes to become more involved in government.

- Periander of Korinthos ruled Corinth and brought stability to the area which had been tormented by conflict.

This isn't the place to list the whole 147 maxims, and it isn't correct to treat them as laws or ethical rules. If you don't follow them, you won't be messing up or facing any retribution, and some of them are considered archaic by today's standards. For example, maxim 94 tells us to "Rule your wife," so good luck with that one!

Some of the More Recognizable Maxims

8. Know Yourself

27. Practice what is just

28. Be kind to your friends

47. Speak well of everyone

56. Down look no-one

60. Be jealous of no-one

73. Be happy with what you have

92. Finish the race without shrinking back

101. Repent of sins

105. Guard friendships

113. Accept old age

118. Do not abandon honor

126. Respect the elder

127. Teach the youngster

132. Die for your country

147. Reach the end without sorrow

The most interesting thing to notice is just how relevant the language of the Maxims is, even though they were written over seven thousand years ago.

The ancient Greeks were forward-thinking and believed in the same morals and guidelines we have today.

Hellenic faith is based on both written and oral history, and the Delphic Maxims can be observed at the Temple of Apollo in the corridor that leads to the main hall.

Conclusion

As you come to the end of your Hellenic journey, it becomes clear that ancient Greece was a land of many facets. The people were educated, and women were encouraged to be more involved in society and religion. How different is it from today? Are the ancient Pythia the first form of information access that we all look for? Is it really different from our current information sources? How many times have you used Google or other Internet sources to check your facts or ask questions? We regularly use information that has come from a remote source without knowing exactly where it originated from, so are we so far removed from the pilgrims who traveled to Delphi and other sacred sites to get the answers they needed?

We may scoff at ancient ways, but does that mean we can't learn from them? The Delphic Maxims are still relevant today, and this just shows us that we aren't that different from the Greeks, who just wanted to live a better life. Good luck on your journey, and I hope you have enjoyed your Hellenic experience.

References

"Delphi Timeline." Www.worldhistory.org, www.worldhistory.org/timeline/delphi/.

"Delphic Maxims." Hellenic Faith, 15 Nov. 2017, hellenicfaith.com/delphic-maxims/.

Editor, The. "Delphi, a Brief History of the "Navel of the Earth."" Thedelphiguide.com, thedelphiguide.com/category/delphi-history/.

---. "The History of Delphi Archaeological Museum." Thedelphiguide.com, 28 Apr. 2017, thedelphiguide.com/the-history-of-delphi-archaeological-museum/.

---. "The History of Delphi Archaeological Museum." Thedelphiguide.com, 28 Apr. 2017, thedelphiguide.com/the-history-of-delphi-archaeological-museum/.

Hayward, Laura. "Oracle of Delphi: Why Was It so Important to Ancient Greeks?" TheCollector,

29 Nov. 2020, www.thecollector.com/oracle-of-delphi/.

"Sanctuary of Apollo | Delphi, Greece Attractions." Lonely Planet, www.lonelyplanet.com/greece/delphi/attractions/sanctuary-of-apollo/a/poi-sig/1518332/359462.

"The Most Famous Oracles of Pythia." GHD, www.greecehighdefinition.com/blog/the-most-famous-oracles-of-pythia.

UNESCO World Heritage Centre. "Archaeological Site of Delphi." Unesco.org, 2012, whc.unesco.org/en/list/393.

"What Lies Beneath: The Great Excavation SACRED DELPHI." GHD, www.greecehighdefinition.com/blog/2021/3/2/what-lies-beneath-the-great-excavation-sacred-Delphi.

Printed in Great Britain
by Amazon